T0195850

Every Ocean

Legends of the Mermaid

Inspired by true events from the journals
of Joseph Wayne Williams

To order additional copies of this book, contact:
Xlibris
844-714-8691
www.Xlibris.com
Orders@Xlibris.com

ISBN: Softcover   979-8-3694-0442-3
       Hardcover   979-8-3694-0443-0
       EBook   979-8-3694-0444-7

Library of Congress Control Number: 2023914249

Print information available on the last page

Rev. date: 08/16/2023

Every Ocean
Legends of the Mermaid

About the Book   Inspired by true events

Open your hearts and souls, as you travel Wayne's unique and magical journey through his powerful and true journals. Unfolding all across the peninsula of Florida and in the warm water of every ocean. As Wayne works spear fishing, he finds the ocean will soon provide more than just a living. Keeping this secret since 1976, over forty years, Wayne has not spoke a word. Now 2023 Wayne opens his journals for the world to see. Two-women, one Mermaid, Two true love stories and the secret code. Written in Haiku-Poetry and hidden within the words of Wayne's journal this secret code reveals itself. Although many may read Wayne's journals only those who possess a pure heart, pure soul and steadfast love, have the ability to unlock the secret code. As you turn the pages in disbelief witnessing the pure heart, soul and steadfast love of Wayne's, as it brings life to the myth and legend. Watch as Wayne dances on the beach sand in the cool surf with the mermaid shadow.

The World
Now Knows

Every Ocean
Legends of the Mermaid

About the Author
Inspired by true events

(Joseph Wayne Williams) Born February 3rd,1959 on the Southeast shores of the peninsula now known as Florida in a small town with a tropical environment know as North Miami Beach at North Shore Hospital. Shortly after my arrival on 2/3/59, I was introduced to my family Fred (Dad) Pearl (Mom) Freddy (Brother) in a few short years the magical flight of the stork would deliver Jackie (Sister). Although I loved and have a loving family, Jackie and I share a powerful and unique bond. Unknowing to me through many years yet understanding as life went on Jackie was sharing her pure heart, Prue soul and steadfast love while teaching me the true gift of life, that would eventually allow me to unlock the legend and myth showing the world Majestic Mermaids do exist. Jackie was in fact the original Majestic Magical and Beautiful mermaid. Possessing the ability to take the form of different women yet remain the same, allowing her to travel through time, sharing her knowledge and truth of life as she has since the beginning of time.

The World
Will Soon Know

Every Ocean
Legends of the Mermaid

Table of contents

Every Ocean
Legends of the Mermaid

Chapter 1,
First Sighting

If I recall correctly the year was 1976, 17 years old and way ahead of my times. I was spearfishing in the Gulf of Mexico, somewhere between Polie Ridge and dry Tortugas. It was Thursday November 4th, YES!! November 4th, 1976, damn it, it's been 44 years ago to the day. Spearfishing in around 97 feet of water visibility was great, could see clearly for a long distance, last dive of the day when I saw a flash out of the corner of my eye. As I turned, and swam closer to look, the figure moves farther and deeper into the ocean. My dive tank becoming very low on air, I knew I must return to the boat, as I began my ascent to the surface this figure appeared once again, THE SILHOUETTE OF A MERMAID!!, I was startled as I heard many tales of this through the years. Returning to my boat I marked this location on my chart.

Swearing Never To Tell Anyone

Every Ocean
Legends of the Mermaid

Chapter 2,
Quest of a Lifetime

After my first sighting Thursday November 4th,1976, I returned many times to this dive site in hopes of another encounter with the majestic and beautiful mermaid. The years unfold with no sighting at that dive site or any other dive site. Now Monday November 4th, 1996, twenty years have passed, although I've never seen her again, I've always hoped and knew she was swimming just out of sight. I am diving at alligator reef lighthouse in the Florida Keys, latitude 24.8518 N longitude 80.6189 W, this lighthouse is located four nautical miles east of Indian key, near Matecumbe keys in the Atlantic Ocean. Spearfishing having a productive day, lots of big fish, sitting on the port side of my boat enjoying the end of a wonderful day. I feel something brush against the haul of my boat, when I looked, I heard the splash, THE BEAUTIFUL TAIL OF THE MERMAID!!! I jumped in the water only to see the delineation of the mermaid, not having my dive tank, I could not give chase, I watched as she disappeared once again into the depth of the ocean.

Still Swearing Never To Tell Anyone

Every Ocean
Legends of the Mermaid

Chapter 3,
Whispering Fish House

Nestled in the Florida Keys at mile marker 47 on marathon key, lies marathon fish house open first in 1967. Due to the location of my lobster and stone crab business, this is where I first sold and still do all of my seafood bounty, they open anytime I call, they buy everything that I catch or shoot. Tuesday November 4th, 2008, pulling up to the dock with hopes of a large payday. Very tired and weak as I have been offshore spearfishing for the past four days. While sitting waiting my turn to unload my weight of seafood, I overheard the word mermaid from down the dock. I moved closer to this crowd eavesdropping on their conversation, I was amazed at what they were Speaking of, YES, A MERMAID SIGHTING!!! I listened good the sighting was at Cosgrove shoal light longitude 8148.1 W latitude 24.27 5 N located 20 miles W.S.W. of key west, south of the Marquesas keys. I unloaded my fish, received my check, on the way back to my boat I asked a man if he saw the mermaid, the most beautiful thing he has ever seen was his reply. Not a word I spoke of my encounters or love for this majestic beauty hoping he would never tell anyone.

Once Again Swearing Never To Tell Anyone

Every Ocean
Legends of the Mermaid

Chapter 4,

Planning the pursuit of the Mermaid

Having remembered the location I heard about at marathon fish house in regards to a mermaid sighting, I recall this dive site as I have dove it many times Cosgrove shole light, technology has advanced greatly since I have been diving, now armed with the Garmin 13 GPS locating a dive spot and returning to the exact location is very simple today is Wednesday January 7th, 2009 the wind is blowing out of the northwest at 37 knots far too rough to pursue the mermaid or even spearfish productively, weather advisories insist it will be like this for the next few days. I spend my time repairing lobster and stone crab traps, tuning my motor making minor repairs. Unable to get the mermaid off my mind even for a moment, I decide researching the myth of the mermaid would be the best way to spend my time, achieving a more vivid understanding of the mermaid and her majestic beauty.

Still Swearing Never To Tell Anyone

Every Ocean
Legends of the Mermaid

Chapter 5,
Research reveals the magic and
the myth of the Mermaid

Research has opened my eyes, the earliest mermaid legend recorded was around 1000 BC in Syria. Atargatis who was the goddess of fertility dove into a lake and begin to take the form of a fish, out of shame for accidentally killing her human lover. With the beauty of her so powerful and majestic, the gods would only allow her lower body to take the form of a fish leaving her from the waist up in human form to retain her beauty. Since these times many of us have grown up with mermaids in books, movies even as toys. Many like myself are drawn to the magically and majestic beauty of this creature. Like me for others it has led to a lifetime search. Knowing the public and people are followers for the most part, Disney movies used a magical story by Hans Christian Andersen 1836 to bring a worldwide phenomenon of mermaids to our homes as treasured fantasies, through TV's and books the myths and majestical beauty of mermaids is not isolated as they have been sighted in every ocean.

Still Never To Tell Anyone

Every Ocean
Legends of the Mermaid

Chapter 6,
Weather clears the pursuit Continues

Not able to pursue the mermaid since Wednesday January 7th, 2009, due to weather conditions. I have done many hours of research on mermaids today is Tuesday January 13, 2009, weather has calmed down. I'm heading to Cosgrove shole light just east of Sugarloaf key the location I heard about on the docks at marathon fish house by other fishermen. Arriving at my dive site longitude 81.189682 1 W latitude 24.691402 N which was easy to locate due to my Garmin GPS. Spearfishing as I do to make a living, I still find myself preoccupied with the thought of locating the mermaid. The day winding down plenty of fish in the cooler, I wonder if I will ever encounter the beautiful mermaid again. Deciding to move to shallower water and spear some fish for dinner, I jump into the shallow warm water, I am on edge my heart started beating faster and faster, YES, THE MAJESTIC MERMAID!!! She swims closer than ever before, I could see her eyes, her scales were like velvet she was more beautiful than I imagined. I could not move or speak, she seemed puzzled by this, as she swam off disappearing once again into the depth of the Atlantic. Somehow, I now feel she knows my infatuation of her extraordinary beauty, she overwhelms my complete existence and powers me to find a way to speak with her. I climb into my boat finding it hard to leave this location, I start my motors term West heading back towards the docks. At this moment I look up at the clouds only to see the clouds in the shape of a mermaid, tears of enchantment blurred my vision I take pause before continuing back towards the docks.

Still Swearing Never To Tell Anyone

Every Ocean
Legends of the Mermaid

Chapter 7,
Was it only a Dream!

Well as all things do, fishing has become difficult to make a living, new rules and regulations have made it tough if not impossible to stay in the keys. Having been through electrical school, I will open a new chapter in my life, I'll start by moving back to the mainland Fort Lauderdale FL. Today is Saturday October 17, 2015, sold my lobster boat and all traps. Will start packing up for a move although letting go of a life in paradise, living off the grid not ever worrying what time or what day it was will truly be a drastic disappointment. All of these things were no sacrifice compared to leaving the beautiful perhaps only a dream of the majestic mermaid. As I have not seen her since Tuesday January 13th, 2009, this has been over six years ago I watched the sunset disappear at the West End of Duval St in the Florida Keys I bid the mermaid farewell I start my quest on a new journey in life.

Still Never To Tell Anyone

Every Ocean
Legends of the Mermaid

Chapter 8,

Unhappy on the Mainland

Leaving paradise Saturday October 17th, 2015, this has been over two years ago as today is Friday November 10th, 2017. I feel lost cannot focus on anything for very long I have been going in circles, as every thought leads me back to her YES, THE BEAUTIFUL MERMAID!!! now with a house, electrical company (JW enterprises) holding its own I will begin looking for a boat. Without enough money to order a new boat I will put the word out to friends, I'm in the market for a center console, single outboard 24 to 26 foot with trailer available for around 8 to $12,000. I find myself spending more and more time at the beach from cocoa beach South to Hollywood beach. I go at all different times in hopes of any sign of her, wondering if she was real or just my over infatuated imagination. I will never stop searching for her, I will borrow my friends wave runner this coming weekend. Must find a way to speak with her, I feel she is just out of sight and understands I'm searching for her.

Still Have Not Told Anyone

Every Ocean
Legends of the Mermaid

Chapter 9,
Reef # 2 Dania Beach

Saturday November 11th, 2017, now 6:32 AM, 68 degrees very cool and calm morning, having borrowed Robert's wave runner to spend the day at and around John Lloyd Park at Dania beach Florida, pretending to be having fun with friends. My real reason for going today is to search for the majestical beauty that I am drawn to, YES, THE MERMAID!!! now 10:37 AM have been spending the morning with friends playing frisbee and horseshoes in the beach sand under the tall pine trees at John Lloyd Park. I've decided to take a ride on the wave runner down the intercoastal out of Fort Lauderdale inlet back South towards Dania Beach Oceanside of John Lloyd Park. Running the intercoastal slowly watching everything going on, boat after boat full of people enjoying their day. I often wonder with this many people enjoying the ocean has anyone ever seen mine or any other mermaid, perhaps I'm crazy. Having bought a mask, fins and snorkel I decided to snorkel at the third reef just South of the jetties. The water is nice around 62 degrees very calm, still low tide about 38 feet deep, has been many years since I dove this area. The reef looked sick lots of dead fennel and antler coral I am disgusted with what I see. As I swam South with the current, I find some spots that still have live coral, more sand and nurse sharks than anything a few lobsters, some small grouper, and a large school of yellowtail swim by me.

Now 11:48am tide changes around 12:30 or so, I'm heading to the South end of Dania Beach and dive 2nd reef, I put four dumpsters there many years ago to make artificial reefs. Current is strong at this location; I will hold on to a rope tied to the wave runner and let the current pull me and the wave runner. An hour has passed with the second reef more alive than the third reef. I'm enjoying this swim wondering if I will ever encounter the beautiful mermaid again, I see a shadow above me close to the wave runner as I turned to see, it as if a spell has been cast over me the mermaid is holding on to the wave runner pulling me towards her with the rope I am holding. I am so astonished I let go of the rope the current is pulling me farther from her, not strong enough to swim against the current I relax and drift away. Suddenly I feel a soft and magical hand grasp my arm, this feels like a dream everything is moving in slow motion, I am now face to face with my lifelong quest the MERMAID!!! she pulls me with ease to the side of the wave runner. I am speechless and stunned I reach and touch her beautiful face as she smiles. Her eyes are pure, skin of silk, and lips of passion. I stared at her with the seaweed top across her breast. I can't stop myself I reach out and begin to touch her complete body, as to my disbelief her lower body does not feel like scales but so wonderfully smooth like powder. I pull myself close to her she does the same, there was a mental orgasm between us that explodes with dynamic feelings only lovers could ever know of. With the slap of her tail, she is gone once again. I was captivated, as the tiny bubbles from the slap of her tail seemed to spell out, YOUR COMPELLING LOVE HAS SOLIDIFIED OUR DESTINY. I spend a moment pulling myself together, and start the run back to John Lloyd Park, load the wave runner and head home. No longer wondering if she understands the powerful and resolved love, I have for her. I now acknowledge that she is my compass in life my true north.

Swearing Never To Tell Anyone

Every Ocean
Legends of the Mermaid

Chapter 10,

Ocean breeze Speaks

Now Friday March 16th, 2018, cold morning at 49 degrees the high will be around 89 degrees today. Electric work has been keeping me off the water since Saturday November 11th, 2017. I go to the north end of Dania Beach, and walk out on the jetties from time to time, as the wind blows the waves through the rocks of the jetties, I find myself mesmerized perhaps even hypnotized, I can hear her YES THE INTRIGUING MERMAID!!! speaking to me. Not caring about the people fishing from the rocks, I find myself talking with her. Strangely a young girl approaches me, perhaps four or five years old, she asks who were you speaking with Sir, I replied why, she said she could hear a lady speaking but does not see her. I asked her what she heard the lady say, the little girl stuttered and said she thought she heard the lady say every ocean, I CRIED AND HUGGED HER FOR SHE TOO COULD HEAR THE MERMAID.!!! As I was leaving the jetties her parents approached me asked me for my phone number, their daughter must hear the story of Wayne's mermaid, not giving my number but taken there's I was not ready to share any of this at this time perhaps another time.

Asking The Little Girl And Her
Parents Never To Tell Anyone

Every Ocean
Legends of the Mermaid

Chapter 11,
Overdue Engagement

After several times and countless hours spent on the Dania beach jetties wondering if this is her, I'm hearing, or just my overactive imagination. From time to time, I can hear her so very clearly as we talk through the night, I am planning to go back to the jetties Saturday March 10th, 2018. Financially unable to purchase a boat, I now have a wave runner. I will spend the complete day on the water (weather permitting) not sure what I am in store of, I know it is time to embrace and face my fears of this only being a concoction of my magnificent imagination, or the majestic beauty I've been in search of, for many years. At any rate I must know with uncertainty one way or the other if this majestic and beautiful mermaid is authentic or only a myth.

Still Swearing Never To Tell Anyone

Every Ocean
Legends of the Mermaid

Chapter 12,
Within the Wake

Now Sunday March 11th, 2018, being sure to move my clocks ahead, as not to miss a moment of tomorrow. Although temperature will be in the high 40s and low 50s the sun will be up, I am hoping the cold weather will keep most boats out of the water tomorrow. As I turn south on the wave runner and past between the jetties, I find the ocean as flat as a lake, the water is beautiful. I wonder when our paths will cross again?? Running about 1/2 mile offshore around 55 miles an hour I leave a very small wake beside my wave runner. Running south putting the port side of my wave runner to the east, with the sun rise illuminating my wake she appears YES, THE BEAUTIFUL MERMAID!!! As to be gliding in the wake of my wave runner. I am careful but I slow down to give larger wake knowing this will ease her ride in the wake. I slow to a stop now sitting sideways on the seat she pulls herself to the hull of my wave runner crossing her arms and resting her head on them. We have a beautiful conversation without ever saying a word, I slide off the wave runner into the cool ocean waters of the Atlantic.

The beautiful mermaid still resting her head on her arms, I wrap myself around her from behind her and begin whispering in her ear a beautiful story, unknowing at this time it would be one of many that I whisper to her through the many years to come. Never saying a word either one of us the most beautiful thing I've ever imagined I knew only then what the phrase this magic moment means. It was 8:21 AM it felt like only a few minutes when she moved and smiled, I looked, and it was 5:32 PM nine hours my God I'm not sure what happened I can only tell on you it was truly amazing and the kind of loving and bonding that only God's or true lovers will ever embrace. We look in each other's eyes saying farewell for now without ever speaking a word I watched once again as she disappeared into the depths of the Atlantic. I feel now I must tell someone perhaps I will call the little girl from the Dania Beach jetties.

Unsure As To Tell Anyone

Every Ocean
Legends of the Mermaid

Chapter 13,
Enchanting Revelation

Saturday April 21st, 2018, 91 degrees scattered thunderstorms. As cold weather gives way to the hot muggy days of summer and afternoon showers. I find myself dock side at the banana boat Bar and Grill on the intercoastal in Fort Lauderdale FL. Meeting a lifetime friend to grab lunch before heading to fish house, to sell my fish. As I'm enjoying a banana daiquiri, I take notice of a very beautiful and comfortably familiar woman a few tables away, I take my drink move to my boat sitting on the dive platform enjoying the day. I hear a soft voice say hello can I join you I reply yes and help her on my boat, over the transom, to the dive platform. I sit with my feet in the water. As she begins to sit, she puts my hand on the thigh of her leg as she sits while her feet and legs enter the intercoastal waters. I watched in amazement and felt her lower body take the form of a mermaid. I knew there was something about her we talked as if we knew each other forever. Emotions were running wild, that moment I knew she was the luxurious and beautiful mermaid I have searched for many years. I hear my name! as I look up see my friend Dave, I noticed the mermaid slides off the teak dive platform into the water, she vanished once again. While sliding from the teak dive platform of my boat a large scale pulled from her side. I can still feel her presence see her beautiful smile and silly grin every time I touch this scale. Dave says he's not sure what he seen that day slide into the water from my dive platform and has never spoke of this again.

As For Me Still Swearing
Never To Tell Anyone

Every Ocean
Legends of the Mermaid

Chapter 14,
Top Prize at Fishing Tournament
Awards Ceremony

Once again, I find time passes faster and faster, it's a beautiful day Sunday April 25, 2021, I'm attending a fishing tournament awards ceremony in Fort Lauderdale this has arranged seating I find myself in the company of an extremely outspoken young woman who is involved in the fishing tournament who was seated at the same table. Amazingly we find ourselves enjoying the company of each other she holds a special beauty about her that I find wonderfully attractive to me, we spend the remainder of the event together laughing and talking we seem to both be enjoying the long overdue pleasant company of each other, with a lot in common the advent winds down we exchange phone numbers. Never losing complete thought of the powerful love I possess for the majestic mermaid I feel as if I find myself in need of companionship in life to share a conversation viewpoint just life in general. Somehow I must have fell short to fully captivate the beautiful mermaids complete attention, she seems to be content with sharing just enough of her time to keep me intrigued, I am a simple man with very little to offer in the ways of furs and jewels it is the simple things that I have grown to value, above all it's time that you are willing to give to one another, this to me is the most prized currency, (ONES TIME) perhaps I'm procrastinating and wasting both are time but surely the beautiful mermaid holds no proclivity as my intentions are honorable as to spend a lifetime with her.

For her existence depends completely on my powerful and unwavering belief and love of her. I have a strange feeling about the woman that I've spent the afternoon with somehow it seems we belong together. I will put my needs of companionship aside until my next encounter with the powerful majestic and beautiful mermaid as I walk up the steps of the grand entranceway to the auditorium that held this event something urges me to turn and as I look back across the crowded auditorium she was also looking and waving she seems to have been keeping an eye out for me as well. Fueled by legends and myths it is my understanding a mermaid can take on different forms of a woman and remain the same. As she waved and said goodnight it was only then that her beautiful smile and silly grin gave her away, she was in fact the beautiful mermaid YES, MORE BEAUIFUL THEN BEFORE.

Have I questioned my steadfast love of
the mermaid (I THINK NOT)
For only she could have held my attention for so long.

Swearing Never To Tell Anyone

Every Ocean
Legends of the Mermaid

Chapter 15,
Flickering Candlelight

Having had time to reflect on the events that unfolded Sunday during the fishing awards ceremony, regarding the all too short time I had spent with the atypical and all so beautiful mermaid. Today is Monday April 26th, 2021. I'm in Tarpon Springs located on the West Coast of Florida I'm involved with one of my electrical projects I find myself and my crew being off early as the project is not ready for the wall rough electrical installation. It is a beautiful day 77 degrees clear and breezy deciding to look around the local waterways, I end up at a place known as the sponge docks checking out the boats and spending a day talking to local fishermen and divers. Now 5:38 PM I head over to the rusty belly waterfront grill which was recommended by several locals. It is a laid-back family-owned tiki bar and grill on the water with live music. I walked through the restaurant out to the dock side tables; I find myself not at all surprised to see the delightful and captivating mermaid. She has a table for two She seems to have had consideration when choosing a table close enough to the band to enjoy the music, just far enough away from the band where we can enjoy each other's conversation.

Not finding it strange to cross paths with her at this location, as somehow, we seem to find each other in the enormous open waters of every ocean. We enjoy a fantastic dinner with the most tranquil and meaningful conversation I have ever imagined possible. As the sunsets the waitresses light the candles on the tables and the tiki torches up and down the docks, as the sax player takes to the stage blowing beautiful music through her saxophone. I am across the table facing the majestic mermaid holding her left hand with my right hand. As she is sipping her iced tea, I am looking at how astonishingly beautiful she truly is with the full moon behind her and the flickering of the candlelight. As it rectifies her already unprecedented beauty. At that time her unprecedented beauty becomes innovatively alive and overwhelms me. I move from across the table and sit beside her. I try my best to tell on her how many ways I love her and how exceptionally wonderful this evening has been. Respectfully she excuses herself to take a phone call.

I have now become perplexed as she does not return. I pay the tab and the waitress asked is everything OK with your lovely friend. I reply, perhaps she has disappeared once again back into the comforting warm waters of the Gulf of Mexico. The waitress odd smile told me she to truly understands as she witnessed the powerful and intertwinement of our pure love and souls.

Requesting to the waitress please never tell anyone

Every Ocean
Legends of the Mermaid

Chapter 16,
From Calm Waters Becomes Balance

I AWAKE!!! pondering the very peculiar ending to the wonderful evening that the beautiful mermaid and I enjoyed last night. It is now 3:00 AM I find myself up early having a few hours before my busy day of work is to begin. I decided to run up and get some coffee before I know it, I am parked at the sponge docks in front of the fishing charter boats in the calm of the morning. Walking along the docks looking down the deep-water canal. With the dock lights from each house lighting up the dark and flat waterway, every ripple on the water catches my eye I am filled with excitement and anticipation in hopes of crossing paths with the enchanting and also beautiful mermaid. Not knowing if I was to question her unusual departure last night or tell her thank you and what a remarkable evening, I enjoyed with her. One last look down the uninterrupted peaceful waterway, I will head to work and wrap myself around the project for the day. While it seems, the day ended all too soon, I eagerly grasp my thought of how much I enjoy my job. I seem to enjoy it as passionately and with equal excitement and enthusiasm that overwhelms me when in the presence of the enchanting mermaid. Is it possible that I have achieved the unobtainable and sought-after balance of life, that has eluded many for years. Somehow someway with each encounter we share together another door opens that brings a level of harmony into my life, in such a way that allows me to understand and able to accept my new view of life and the true gift that life is. No longer do I wonder; I have achieved the understanding what the true meaning is all about. (THE TRUTH WILL SET YOU FREE) somehow, she has given me the ability of learning not to question, only to understand all life for what it truly is.

Somehow, she finds a way to share with me her wisdom she has achieved through centuries of roaming every ocean.

Swearing Never To Tell Anyone

Every Ocean
Legends of the Mermaid

Chapter 17,
Silent Gift of Inheritance
Friday September 23, 2022

Up early as is my routine, I spent the next hour writing my mom a letter, just a note perhaps letting her know how much I love her and what a nice time I had spending the day with her. I find myself elated for her to take interest in knowing something about the book I am writing. (This should not puzzle you it is this book you're reading now). We spend the better part of the morning sitting at her table in a dimly lit dining room. I gave my foremost effort while answering her questions on how and where this story has unfolded within me. As she reads through my book a 2 true, powerful and beautiful love story. I explain I am confident through this book I am able to express the also powerful connection of life and pure love that the mermaid and I have been gifted with. I can feel her overwhelming joy that her son has somehow stumbled on the gift of true love and life with all of its pure meaning. For she too has been one of the few who had the honor and privilege of a lifetime enjoying the true experience of this phenomenal gift. As everyone knows Pearl and Fred were undoubtfully matched by some remarkable power from above, they truly traveled through an enchanting lifetime together. Somehow, I feel my mother finds a comforting and peaceful feeling knowing I also will experience this wonderful gift that all too few will ever know of or that it even existed. I think to myself what a wonderfully remarkable day this has been. As today is surely another precious and priceless memory passed from a parent to a child. I FIND MYSELF FORTUNATE TO HAVE BEEN THIS CHILD.

The World Already Knows

Every Ocean
Legends of the Mermaid

Chapter 18,
Solidified Beliefs

I find myself back in Tarpon Springs, FL. as I went through electrical wall rough inspection today, I passed, although the inspector had a few comments on the inspection card small items knocked out seals missing, two blank covers not marked and some strapping in a few locations. We corrected these items and took the rest of the day off. We all went back to our motel rooms cleaned up; I am taking the crew out this evening for dinner. Being as it was a planned engagement, we will meet at captain Jacks Bar and Grill, located at 21 Oscar hill Rd. Tarpon Springs. This is a nice place tropically themed with a fantastic seafood menu. Although dock side tables are available, we decide to eat inside with the comfort of air condition and no mosquitoes. We had a wonderful dinner and fantastic time; we will be off for the next few days waiting on the drywall contractor to finish their work. Some of the crew will head home to spend the next few days with their families which is well deserving. I will stay at the motel, order material schedule the task for the next few days coming. I also look forward to looking around the island and enjoying the local culture. As we say our goodbyes and the crew disperses, I thank every member of Team Kodiak for their hard work and friendship, I grab a cold beer head Outback standing on the dock looking up and down the waterway I see a boatyard a working boatyard the sign reads Pittman yacht service this will be a must see for tomorrow.

Arriving back at my motel I decided to research Pittman yacht service they have been in business over 25 years they're located at 1058 Island Ave Tarpon Springs on the Anclote River across from sponge docks their travel lift can handle yachts up to 75 tons with a 20-foot beam this is very impressive. 4:07 AM having slept well, I am thrilled in knowing I am on my way to explore a working full-service boatyard if you know anything about boats you can understand my excitement and prolepsis, I stopped for a cup of coffee and buy some beef jerky. Coffee I will drink, the beef jerky is for the yard dog I am expecting to encounter. As every boat yard I have been too has a yard dog, and most times they're not eager to make friends. Pulling up to the locked gate at Pittman yacht service and yes, some kind of mixed mutt, with a mouth like a 5-gallon bucket and teeth that look like railroad spikes and surely weighs well over 100 pounds. Before I get out of my truck, I write a note as to my presence in the boatyard taping the note to the fence post,

As the mutt has all but eaten the gate, his way of introducing himself perhaps. Someone is surely watching over me as I seem to have bought the correct flavor of beef jerky the mutt and I bond for a moment, then I slipped myself between the chained gates. As I walked past all the factories made and cookie cutter boats towards the back of the boat yard suddenly the smell of the boatyard is screaming with fiberglass, teakwood, gelcoat, bottom paint and pure sweat of the true sculptures who create these unique vessels these are the vessels, in which the ocean brings life to as it also does for the mermaid. I stopped for a moment giving the mutt more jerky.

Suddenly my mind is completely clear of any thoughts. I paused for a moment, my father comes to my mind so powerful I can feel his presence, as he was truly one of these sculptures who created a beautiful boat, as I witnessed on its maiden voyage when it first touched the ocean water, to my disbelieve the vessel was given life. Somehow my father is in my heart at this moment, also enjoying this time we seem to be spending together. As I believe he lives through me and me through him. All the handmade boats are beautiful each one is surely a sculpture with the distinctive curves and characteristics that the sculptor incorporates as he builds. With the understanding that a boat builder incorporates the curves of the women they love in each handmade boat. I would imagine each individual vessel becomes their image of their floating mermaid.

The vessel, boat, sculpture or floating mermaid which Fred designed and built and all its distinctive curves and the characteristics of a Princess, justifying its beauty with the name Pearl, who was Fred's only love.

Now standing on a dock style boat slip on the waterway at Pittman yacht service I am looking at a large sport fishing boat it is suspended and hanging by large straps from the travel lift as in preparation of being lowered into the water perhaps on its maiden voyage. Vessels of this stature seem to be giving life the first and every time they collied with ocean waters as mermaids do and have since the beginning of time. Splashing from under the dock catches my attention. I look to see a school of baitfish jumping around, looking closer I see her reflection YES, THE MERMAID!!! Standing behind me. She takes my hand and helps me stand, I put my arms on her waist she puts her arms on my shoulders I find myself stuttering with excitement explaining what a great morning I have had. She smiles and replies, as your father, I too have spent the day with you. Your father also a legend and a gentle and understanding man she adds. How or why, she knew this, I did not ask. As she has never met him before. With sunrise approaching I was glad to see workers showing up, I have ran out of jerky for the mutt. As an older man approaches us introducing himself as skip and announcing his employment here, I introduced the mermaid and myself after some interesting conversation pertaining to the amazingly and remarkable boatyard. I asked about the mutt he laughed and replied that's dusky he just barks he has never bit anyone. The mermaid looks at me with her amazing silly grin, she giggles fooled by a mutt (I smiled). Escorting her to our truck we retreat to the comfort of our motel and lock ourselves in for the evening.

She Requests That I Never Tell Anyone

Chapter 19,
Company of Purity

Although the electrical project in Tarpon Springs is winding down. I will not soon forget, all the wonderful people and places that the mermaid and I have had the pleasure of enjoying together. Having been another true testimony of our companionship and collective interests while exploring life together. Another quality project behind us. Passing final electrical inspection, corrected a few items at the owner's request. Now heading back to the motel, I stopped for grilled shrimp on skewers in hopes my mermaid will eat. Knowing she is well rested as I did not wake her this morning, leaving her with fresh fruit and whispering an extremely beautiful story in her ear, then kissing her soft lips before heading to work. Upon arriving from work to our motel, she greets me in the lobby, so beautiful as she is. Her delightful smile and gorgeous bathing suit. She is impressively lovely as her body appears to have been kissed by the sun. She goes on to explain what a nice day she spent on the beach and poolside. Also having enjoyed lunch and interesting conversation with some of the local residents. I hit the shower while she ate very little as expected. I finished some closeout documents for my project, requesting her to escort me out for the evening for ice cream at sprinkles ice cream parlor located at the sponge docks, I throw on shorts and a short sleeve button up polo shirt, she emerges from the bathroom with dazzling beauty her smooth softly tanned body providing a beautiful backdrop for the stunning pale teal mini skirt and sheer white tube top she is breathtaking as always. I need not remind myself, as others do telling me what a lucky man I am. She smiles and reassures me beauty is one's conception and must possess a pure heart and soul. Nothing to do with luck. I kiss her while opening the truck door for her I drift away in the conversation and company of her kindness and cordialness, this will be another eventful and memorable evening as our life together continues to unfold.

Still Telling No One

Chapter 20,
Our Time / True Currency

Tarpon Springs now in our rearview mirror. The mermaid and I will set off in search of some alone down time. Thus, maintaining the balance of life as we understand. Some would believe this is unnecessary and complicated. With our life as it is, we find this conventional. Asking for nothing as she does, she like me finds contentment and the all inspiring time we seem to find within each other. We take turns driving, reading and singing to one another. We often find ourselves singing pictures by Kid Rock and Cheryl Suzanne crow. My voice is horrible as she still enjoys my effort and excitement while singing to her never criticizing. Then her singing starts her voice fills the large cab of our truck with a one-of-a-kind sound of the GeniSys organ from the Vatican complex in Vatican City Rome. Intertwined with the beautiful sound only a choir of angels can produce. She is truly wonderfully amazing looking at me while she is singing. I can not only see her I also feel her with her confidence and beauty as she knows my heart belongs only to her.

Amazing as today has been it is now winding down. I will stop, pick up some food, and find a motel to spend the night in Gainesville, FL. I ran in and grabbed a burger for myself, as I give her a chicken sandwich her silly grin more silly and bigger than ever. I will not mention why, (IF YOU REMEMBER ASK HER AT HER NEXT BOOK SIGNING) perhaps she will share this with you. We eat she gives me that special thank you for the chicken sandwich. Tired as we are, I wrap myself around her from behind telling her goodnight and how wonderful I feel to have her in my life. I whisper yet other beautiful story in her ear before we raise our hands as our fingertips collied, we give thanks realizing the true blessing our love is.

Swearing To Tell No One

Every Ocean
Legends of the Mermaid

Chapter 21,
Greatest Show On Earth

Gainesville was a much overdue relaxing and unwinding time as I awake, I take notice of the mermaid absences, all the while knowing the depths of the ocean continue calling her. I long for the time when her attraction shifts. Change I understand is hard for her, she has been wet for many years, understanding it would be uncomfortable to remain dry. I believe if she finds interest she enjoys, this change will seem less uncomfortable to her. I packed up head to Jacksonville, FL. next electrical project. My office having booked and confirmed a room at Amelia hotel at the beach located at 1997 S. Fletcher Ave, Amelia Island. Arriving I find this motel to be uncomfortably extravagant not having the company of the mermaid. I will look for another hotel in the area with far meager accommodations. I check in then head over to the project at 10051 Skinner Lake Dr Jacksonville, FL. Before existing the lobby, I request a call if a mermaid shows up. The manager gives me a odd and strange look replying yes sir, is that all. The night is calm with a full moon.

Driving down Fletcher Ave on the beach I take notice a restaurant, sliders seaside grill. Pulling in, the place is packed. Walking through the door I can feel the exciting ocean climate this place is jumping. Keyboard and brass band providing soothing music. Not a patient man refusing to wait on hostess to be seated. I find myself a table outside on the deck, looking across the beach sand the moon lighting up the Atlantic Ocean, this suits my comfort. Enjoying a Margarita watching the waves, set after set of smooth rolling ocean water. A disturbance in the water close to shore catches my eye. To my delightful surprise yes, the magnificent mermaid. I take notice of the soft ocean surf as it gently pushes her onto the beach sand, I find myself no longer intimidated of her exquisitely elegant beauty. Knowing our hearts are as one. I remove my shirt and begin to dry her complete body and soft scales. As the ocean waters began drying from her beautiful skin and beautiful smooth and fluorescent blue green scales. I witnessed a spectacular transformation.

Now standing before me barefoot on the beach sand my lifetime companion. With the Atlantic Ocean and full moon behind her magnifying her alluring heart stopping beauty. The ocean breeze combined with the soothing music providing a fairytale atmosphere. She seems confused and appears unable to move, as to be frozen in time. Watching as I reach down on the beach sand and gently take the hand of her shadow. Her shadow follows my lead we began to dance. She watches as her shadow, and I dance to the all enchanting LADY IN RED. This song finished, while returning her shadow she abruptly becomes alert as to have been spellbound. I hugged her before kissing her soft lips I thanked her for the dance.

Once again, her beautiful smile and silly grin says it all, I love you, I whisper in her ear your my forever. We embrace and kiss. All at once extremely loud cheering and clapping destroyed the calm of the moment. A large crowd has gathered as to have been an audience, they are looking as to have been witness to a enchanting, beautiful and unbelievable event. Hand in hand I escort her across the beach sand to the deck of the tiki bar enjoying a nice dinner. Upon leaving not only the owners but many guests, commented as that being the most remarkable and beautiful show they have ever attended, insisting buying our dinner. The mermaid turns to me and smiles. As I gracefully request her company for the evening. We returned to our motel. While wrapped around her from behind, I whisper another beautiful story in her ear. Reminding her she is more beautiful than yesterday.

This Audience Is Sure
To Tell Everyone

Every Ocean
Legends of the Mermaid

Chapter 22,
Silence of Matrimony

Many years have passed, still also vivid and remarkable was that day November 4th, 1976. unknowing to either of us my brief glimpse of her on that special day deep within the ocean waters in the Gulf of Mexico, was to be the beginning of the most wonderful and enchanting lifetime ever to be heard of. Exciting, captivating and delightful were the days that filled our many years that followed and continuing to do so. Having her for my wife I have dreamed and wished for through our many years together. Never asking her, somehow my uncertainty and concern of imposing boundaries and stipulations on the perfect balance in life which our pure love of each other has been our unique and influential bond throughout our many years. Understanding her hand in marriage would express my undivided and honorable commitment of only her. HOW--- WHERE--- WHEN begins consuming my every thought as now I have intentions on asking her.

Suspicious as her mind becomes after I asked her on a date. Her Knowing I am a spontaneous man making very few plans outside of work. She agrees, although she consents. I feel her anxiety of this strange and odd request by me. Satisfying her curiosity Tuesday November 8th three days from now Sliders Seaside Grill, by the way Skip the man from Pittman yacht service is to join us. This day was not a guess as it will provide a full moon with no rain, unknowing to her Skip is a licensed ship captain with the powers to perform wedding vows. Excited as I am the day has arrived, Skip the beautiful mermaid and I having finished a wonderful dinner and conversation. We find ourselves walking on the beach close to the water. She and I remove our shoes walk in the cool water's edge, the moon brighter than ever as I turned to her and dropped to one knee and asked, she screams YES!! OF COURSE, YES!!! Now standing face to face only the ocean mist and moonlight between us. Skip is so amazed I need to remind him why he's here. Clearing his throat assuring her he is a ship captain with the ability to hold witness of matrimony between a man and woman. Holding each other's hands face to face looking deep into one another's eyes reciting our vows to each other never speaking a word. They were the most beautiful and loudest vows ever to be spoken in silence. Not knowing Skip was a soft man he dries his tears I now pronounce you husband and wife Skip recites. I placed a modest mermaid ring on her finger. We raise our hands high in the air allowing our fingertips to softly touch, then kissing her soft lips walking back on the beach sand in the water's edge hand in hand. Whispering in her ear the greatest love story the world has ever known. (OUR STORY)

The World Now Knows

Every Ocean
Legends of the Mermaid

Chapter 23,

Déjà vu

Amazing was that gift of being wed to the captivating mermaid on that extraordinary day. Imagine falling in love every day of your life [As I do] silence as our vows yet still heard around the world were the most explosive words never to be spoken. Exhausted as any man would surely understand, being blessed with the hand of a majestic mermaid. Retiring for the evening, she pulled the sheets back we slide between them. I wrap myself a round her from behind, pulling her soft body tight against mine. Whispering another beautiful and captivating story in her ear, reminding her she has become more charming and beautiful than yesterday. Waking early the alluring mermaid still in my arms, softly I blew across her neck and ear, she sighs while pushing her soft body back against mine. Noticing her ear twitching as I blew on it, I knew she smiled then made that silly grin.

Yawning while asking me if I am working today, [I am] I'm working on making your day more enjoyable and wonderful than yesterday. Squeezing her firmly as I slipped from behind her, I dress and headed out to get breakfast. Having picked up fresh fruit from Publix, now standing in line at Dunkin' Donuts I will pick up glazed blueberry Donuts knowing she favors this. While standing in line I somehow feel the weight of someone's stare, I hear [is that the man that talks to mermaids] I looked back in the line a woman and young girl, both with a very odd look on their face staring at me. I cannot believe it, the little girl from Dania Beach jetties has recognized me. If I recall it was early 2018 over four years ago. The lady requesting, I wait on them. Leaving the store I could see the excitement in the little girl, as she races across the parking lot in my direction. While trying to catch her breath she says hi remember me my name is Aniyah that's my mom Cloe. Her mother approaches and makes introductions. We exchanged phone numbers while I am trying to answer the young girls many questions, about Wayne's majestic mermaid. The lady requesting to please have the mermaid call her daughter I will give her your phone number perhaps she will remember that day on Dania Beach jetties.

Little Girl Sure To Tell Everyone

Every Ocean
Legends of the Mermaid

Chapter 24,
Last Entry Final Voyage (first
of two true love stories)

Now Friday September 2nd, 2022, many years have passed. I've grown tired and old, although my love and passion of the mermaid has dimmed, I still think of her from time to time. Knowing we will never walk together through life; I seem to have lost my infatuation of her somehow her majestic beauty fails to captivate my interest. Her conversation seems to have become flat, repetitive, shallow, tainted and impure. All of the beauty I've found in her is changing her skin is dry, smooth scales have hardened, silly grin and beautiful smile has become a sad frown, her lips are no longer soft and moist they seem to be cracked and discolored, her big bright eyes are now bloodshot with a yellow tent her long beautiful hair is thinning fast and seems to be dying like the coral in the ocean. Even my love could not reverse the damage I will surely miss telling her all of the beautiful stories we've shared. I expect no change as she seems to be swimming in neutral buoyancy, unable to move shallower or deeper from her hateful and destructive thoughts. I however must ascend into reality leaving her as I found her only a myth. Knowing she had been carrying a curse from around 1,000 BC for accidentally killing her human lover. Then she was given the chance to love and be loved she seemed unwilling or unable to accept this gift. Unknowing to her she exists only due to my very powerful belief and love for her. Unaware her existence is fading with each passing unproductive and less enchanting moment we spend together. Perhaps this is because of her lack of drive or unwillingness to put forward any effort in change. She seems to have found comfort with her unhappy and destructive way of life; also seems blind to the fact this will commit her back to the ocean once again. This lifetime quest of the mermaid has been wonderful and unique journey perhaps it was not meant to be. Perhaps she was not the PURE mermaid, at any rate I feel it was not a wasted life.

Swearing Never To Tell Anyone

Every Ocean
Legends of the Mermaid

Chapter 24, Final Entry
Escorted Crossing (Second true love story)

As I feared time is approaching all too fast, my body becomes more fragile and weaker with each passing day. All the while knowing the beautiful mermaid never ages as she is immortal. As I do, she also understands unlike her I was born with an expiration date that is soon to arrive. Although we have frolicked, sang, laughed and cried together through a beautiful but all too short life, we accept the inevitable though never speaking of this. Contrary of our through the sand in the hourglass is a constant reminder there is an end to all beginnings. Just last night while wrapped around one another we found ourselves in search of an explanation as to the unparalleled life we have been blessed with. It is our perception this was due only to my steadfast love and belief of her and the powerful purity she shares so freely not only with me but with every life form on earth, land and sea. As she brings overwhelming joy to all life in which she has contact with. She feels comfortable content and safe as she is falling asleep with her back to me, and me wrapped around her from behind as I whisper another beautiful story in her ear. As I have done for many years, which she has always enjoyed and looks forward to. The stories become more beautiful as she does with each passing night. As we have accepted and known for weeks my life is slipping away. I am aware she forces herself to sleep light as she is attentive to my exhausting laboring of breath as I sleep. I have enjoyed a continuing dream for the past few nights somehow, I find comfort and knowing another man is in line to appreciate the compelling beauty of her purity and love for years after my demise and only imagine the beauty and enhancement she has blessed on others. For she has been around for over 1,000 years sharing her kindness, beauty and knowledge of love through many generations. As I wake suddenly unable to catch my breath or even sit up, I find myself looking into her deep loving eyes, my life is slipping away now I watch as she refuses another breath of life sustaining oxygen and insist on escorting me in my crossing. Somehow, I feel powerfully invincible as not to be afraid of my life slipping away. A brilliant bright light explodes, I feel reborn as I awake with her still wrapped in my arms, was this truly a crossing I wonder or has she willingly giving me the gift of immortality. As to spend eternity by her side.

The Whole World Watches In Amazement!!!

Every Ocean
Legends of the Mermaid
(2)

Chapter 1,
Future Beholds

Many years ago (In the late 80's) holding and looking in my son's eyes I took notice of the remarkable twinkling deep within them. I knew at that moment he too was blessed with the pure heart and soul. Like turning the pages of a book, one by one were the days of his journey unfolding. Meant to be as it was that remarkable day that finally came, the first time their eyes made contact and their hearts collided. They both knew at that moment their destiny and journey together would not be denied. There was no doubt or confusion she was his mermaid (NATALIE), and he (JOEY) was to be her forever. Upon my meeting her for the first time she was truly stunning, her beautiful smile and silly grin altered me she is surely the most majestic mermaid ever to emerge from any ocean. Seeing their calm manner and powerful confidence within each other was not only apparent but it was compelling. Wonderful as a father to witness a son and his mermaid take flight together in their enchanting life. Perhaps unknown to them they are nurturing the next era of mermaids as STERLING, JOEY and ANDIE possess the magical beautiful smile, silly grin and true gift of a pure heart and soul.

Asking the world
To save
EVERY OCEAN

Front cover designed by Miss Jill Cole(Wayne's Aunt)
Back Cover designed by Wayne Williams
Full page Mermaid image by Janet King

Printed in the United States
by Baker & Taylor Publisher Services